The rock pool

Annette Smith
Illustrated by Trevor Ruth

"Look!

We can see

some seaweed."

3

"Look!

We can see

some little shells."

"Look!

We can see

some little crabs."

"Look!

We can see

some little fish."

9

"Look!

We can see

some little starfish."

"Look!

We can see

some little shrimps."

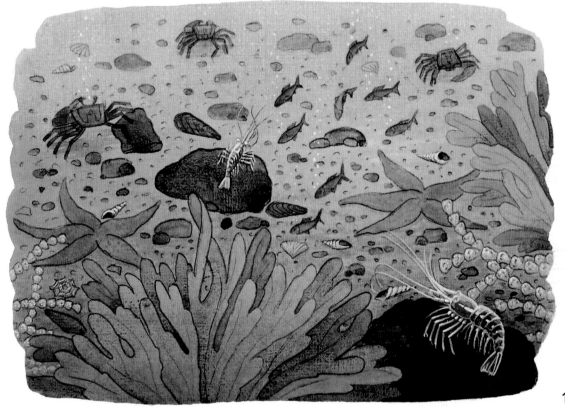

"Look!

We can see

a little ...

... sea horse."